The Life of a Romanian WWI Prisoner of War

A War Journal

by Emma Dirk

 FriesenPress

One Printers Way
Altona, MB R0G 0B0
Canada

www.friesenpress.com

ISBN
978-1-03-830929-7 (Hardcover)
978-1-03-830928-0 (Paperback)
978-1-03-830930-3 (eBook)

1. History, Military, World War I

Distributed to the trade by The Ingram Book Company

Table of Contents

This memoir is dedicated to my remarkable
maternal great-grandfather.

Dumitru Balaci was not just a son, brother, husband, father,
and grandfather, but a source of profound inspiration for
my family, who owes their existence to his never-failing faith
in God, and his adamant determination to come back to his
country and create a legacy for his loved ones.

In loving memory of Dumitru Balaci
(October 18, 1893–1979)

faith

Introduction

Between October 1916 and October 1918, a stunning number of Romanians—43,297, to be exact, consisting of approximately 1,656 officers and 41,641 soldiers—found themselves imprisoned in German camps. The Germans controlled approximately one-third of these Romanian prisoners, while the remaining two-thirds were under the custody of Germany's allies.

After Romania entered the First World War, a considerable number of soldiers, mostly peasants, were captured following the brutal battles in the Carpathians, Oltenia, and Muntenia regions during October and November 1916.

After being transported in cattle trains wrapped with barbed wire, these prisoners experienced a series of brutal treatments enforced by the Germans, including imprisonment, starvation, and torture, resulting in the loss of many Romanian lives between 1917 and 1918. They were locked up in unfinished barracks, enduring the harshness of moist and freezing conditions while guards constantly watched over them. In the daytime, they were tasked with woodcutting and road maintenance, supervised by civilian team leaders. As the winter of 1917 set in, the already difficult conditions for survival in the camp worsened, resulting in many deaths due to hunger and exhaustion.

A wide multitude of events marked the lives of Romanian prisoners of war, from the time of their capture to their eventual downfall, possibly even during the time of their return home. The surviving witnesses of these horrors were profoundly impacted by the ruthless treatment the prisoners of war experienced. To stop future generations from forgetting the bad conditions under which these imprisoned soldiers lived and died, they've put their trust in us with their memories.

Many aspects of Dumitru's life remain covered in mystery, particularly regarding his capture and the precise locations of his imprisonments during the First World War. However, even with these gaps, his journal captures the essence of his experiences, offering a sharp glimpse into his life during those years of suffering.

From the late months of 1916 to the beginning of 1917, Dumitru endured the agonizing ordeal of being a prisoner of war shuffled among multiple concentration camps in Germany and Austria. The constant relocation was disorienting for the prisoners, as they moved to new locations almost monthly. Through his eloquent journal entries, he pointedly reveals glimpses of his daily life in captivity, including the struggle to survive torturous conditions and hunger. In the early spring of 1917, a glimmer of hope became real as Dumitru managed to escape from Salzburg, successfully crossing the border into France.

Based on the journal entries, we discover that he began documenting his experiences from his capture in 1916 until his escape in early 1917. However, he started writing in his journal in the spring of 1917, while in the safety of France, and reflects on the prior year spent as a prisoner of war in Germany and Austria.

Although family accounts are limited, it appears he returned to Romania in 1920–1921 after serving in the French Army for three years. While stationed in France, he had the opportunity to settle there permanently, but his love for family and country, combined with deep roots in his birthplace, made returning home the only viable choice for him.

On the other side of the conflict, he transitioned from captive to comrade, joining the French Army as a soldier fighting alongside the Allies. The entries in his journal, chronicled between 1917 and 1919, unfold a narrative written between the lines of his experiences in France. These emotional inscriptions became a living testament to the recent memories embedded in his mind—a stark contrast to the time spent in captivity in Germany and Austria just a year prior. In the end, the story follows his journey as he finds his way home years later, where he starts a family and leaves behind a legacy—all thanks to the grace of God.

It is my hope that the ink on these pages will breathe life once again into the vivid recollections of his journey from imprisonment to service, capturing the essence of a man who defied the confines of captivity to become a participant on the other side of the battle lines. As his great-granddaughter, while I reflect upon this remarkable journey, I find myself humbled and deeply honoured to be entrusted with immortalizing Dumitru Balaci's experiences in the pages of a book. It is a responsibility I do not take lightly, for his story deserves to be heard and remembered.

Dumitru Balaci

Dumitru Balaci was born in Romania on October 18, 1893. He was the son of Grigore Balaci and lived in Macesu-de Sus, Dolj County, until the age of 23 years old, when his fate took a different turn.

As a prisoner of war, Dumitru was taken hostage on the Oltenia front line and, together with tens of thousands of other Romanians, tolerated a brutal journey on cattle trains to a German concentration camp and was subjected to cruel conditions.

Despite his limited education, due to his rural childhood, where farming was always the priority for his family, Dumitru had a journal. He practised his writing skills on the pages of this journal, starting with the alphabet.

Now, almost 107 years old, the journal remains in an incredibly delicate state. The entries in this journal began in 1917 and continued sporadically until 1919. Dumitru documented his thoughts, love interests, dreams, and daily routines in this journal.

Sometimes, he wrote prayers or simply took notes on the weather, while other times, he would write down a basic grocery list or a list of French words, as if trying to learn them. Some pages have dates at the top, while others have simple inscriptions about the struggles and experiences of a certain day.

Spanning a long period, Dumitru's journal entries vary in writing instruments: sometimes he would use ink, and other times, would write with a pencil. This presented challenges when attempting to decipher the complete context of his entries.

This captivating and extremely personal journal is bestrewn with stories of unimaginable suffering, contrasting with the standards of today's world. Yet, bound by these trials, Dumitru's unshakable love for God and his bold determination to reunite with his family and return to his homeland shine through beyond any doubt.

Inscriptions
1917

January 1917
(Exact Date Unknown)

During our time in Germany, we suffered a lot and we found ourselves imprisoned in a camp, where our daily meals consisted of minimum rations.

Each morning, we would receive a small loaf of bread to share with another five individuals.

We were given beet soup at noon and the same minimal meal was repeated in the evening. These meals, even though they were not much, were all we had to rely on for nutrition.

After surviving the hardships of this camp for one month, we were transported to another location. The journey was gruelling, lasting three long days. Throughout this exhausting train ride, our diet was limited to only two bowls of soup. Hunger was always present, and we hoped for a more substantial diet to take away our physical and emotional hardships.

Finally, the train pulled into a station, signalling our arrival at this unknown new destination. The exhaustion was surreal as

I stepped off the train, and my tired body struggled to make its way through the tough winter terrain. The snow, piled high and harsh, prevailed over me, making me sink into its icy depths, the snow burying me up to my waist.

The cold infiltrated into my very being, further intensifying the immense challenges we had to face while being imprisoned in these camps. These experiences are a testament to the rigid realities we had to endure during our time in Germany, marked by distress, lack of food, exhausting journeys, and the constant struggle against the unforgiving weather during the wintertime.

January 1917
(Exact Date Unknown)

Throughout this year, we found ourselves in a constant state of transition between camps, uncertain if we would ever live to see the light of another day. The harsh reality of our circumstances was carved onto our skeletal bodies, as we constantly lost weight, day and night.

Our existence was reduced to lying in bed, with the only nutrition received being rations of water that came with two hundred grams of bread. The tasteless, repetitive diet did little to help with our hunger, leaving us in a continuous state of physical and mental deprivation. Amid our dire fate, we clung to the hope that the Lord God would deliver us from the burning hell in which we found ourselves.

It is through His divine intervention and providence that we stand here today, having resurfaced from the depths of our suffering.

Our current circumstances, while still far from ideal, have improved considerably from the hopeless existence we endured as prisoners. We recognize that without God's presence and guidance, we would be left with nothing. Our faith in His power has been our reason for strength and resilience throughout these experiences, providing us with the hope and determination necessary to survive against all odds.

1917
(Exact Date Unknown)

Throughout this period of imprisonment, my existence was confined within the unforgiven walls of the camp, where suffering seemed to be my constant partner. It was on the chilly morning of February 10 that we were obligated to go to labour, our bodies were weak and worn. The uphill journey to the worksite proved to be a dreadful task, as our feet struggled to navigate the slippery path laid before us. Each step became an agonizing reminder of our physical and emotional hardships.

For an entire month, we survived in that ruthless environment, our spirits were beaten by the hardships placed upon us.

However, when the time came for us to leave, our destination was a city close to the border with Austria, Salzburg. Little did we know that our circumstances would deteriorate even more upon arrival. As we entered this unfamiliar city, a sense of desolation overcame me, as if we had been transported to an entirely different world.

The conditions we faced there were more unbearable than ever before, intensifying the suffering we had already endured in Germany. However, as time passed, the reality of our situation began to sink in.

Two months later, I caught a glimpse of a few fellow Romanians, but they seemed unrecognizable to me. The toll of suffering had transformed us all, changing our appearances, and our spirits were broken. We had become simple shadows of our former selves, carrying the scars of our collective struggles.

In this surreal state, we found it difficult to identify with one another, as the relentless oppression had destroyed our sense of familiarity and connection. These profound encounters, devastating suffering, and the resulting transformations were a grim reminder of the immense toll it took upon our human spirit.

These scars engraved upon our beings were not only physical but ran deep within, leaving a lasting mark on our sense of identity and our ability to recognize one another amidst the ruins of our shared experiences.

My dearest and beloved Polina, how I long for your presence. In my mind, I dream of you, even though my eyes cannot see your image. When night comes, and sleep overtakes me, I envision you peacefully asleep by my side.

Sleep eludes me, for my thoughts are constantly consumed by our conversations. In the morning, my hunger dissipates as I lay in bed, lost and confused. Polina, where have you been all night? I constantly search for you, longing for your return.

1917
(Exact Date Unknown)

I'm writing this letter as a soldier stationed in France. I long deeply for my parents and for you, my desired mistress, who only exists within the realm of my dreams. Though I have forgotten your appearance, I hold onto the hope that one day, by God's grace, we shall be reunited.

Since I arrived in France, I have taken refuge in the territory liberated from the hands of the Germans, known as Lorraine. Here, I live a quiet life, constantly thinking of my parents. It is for this reason that I have decided not to remain here permanently, for I yearn to witness the situation of our homeland.

If our country has not found peace, I will promptly go wherever God leads me, for our land has been dominated by the greatest of thieves.

However, my time in foreign lands has revealed to me the contrasts between our nations. Our homeland is unlike any other, and I am now aware of the realities that transpire beyond our borders.

> With heartfelt aspiration and undying hope,
> I remain your devoted and affectionate son and soldier,
> Dumitru Balaci of the Infantry

Inscriptions
1918

January 1918
(Exact Date Unknown)

In the realm of divine intervention, the Lord God willed a change to deliver us through our circumstances, bringing with it a spark of hope. It had always been my biggest desire and unshakable expectation to reunite with our French brothers, our brothers-in-arms, and allies, to stand united against the common adversary that was Germany.

Together, we sought to destroy the forces that threatened peace and freedom. With a persistent spirit, we aimed to exterminate the very foundations of Germany's power.

August 1918
(Exact Date Unknown)

Amid the chaos and turmoil, I found myself separated from the comforting presence of my beloved parents and brothers.

Then, I woke up as if I was in a bad dream: I found myself in the relentless explosions of grenades echoing through the air, the fierce chatter of machine guns piercing the silence, and the deafening roar of cannons booming across the battlefield.

As I fought bravely, a part of me yearned for the gentle whispers of the wind bidding farewell to our homeland nestled in the Romanian Carpathians.

In rare moments of pause, when we gathered around the table to eat a meal, our adversaries advanced, disrupting the quietness, and imposing a grim reality upon us. We knew that we could not just sit by while they were ready to come and exterminate us.

With unshakable determination, we abandoned everything on that table, leaving behind half-eaten meals, to confront the imminent threat that was approaching us. Our resolve was unwavering, for we understood that it was through united resistance that we could prevent their sinister intentions from coming to fruition.

In this war, we embraced a common purpose: to fight heroically and relentlessly against our common enemy. Bound together by a common cause, we moved ahead with determination, knowing that our collective strength was the key to destroying the forces that sought to tear us apart.

Let it be a battle waged by all, for together, we will emerge with victory and destroy the enemy that threatens our very existence.

Inscriptions
1919

Early 1919
(Exact Date Unknown)

In the depths of uncertainty and separation, it becomes important to keep you informed of my well-being. Please know that I am in good health and resilient against the trials of war.

However, the situation within the borders of your home remains a mystery to me, leaving me with a sense of disconnection and the unknown. It is in this state of uncertainty that I find myself wondering when our paths will merge once more, for the future holds no certainty or guarantee of being reunited with you. In these moments of longing, I find solace in the pages of books, my intellect shines as I delve into this world of knowledge.

I possess a genuine affection for the company of young women. I particularly love the opportunity to see them on Sundays. My interactions manifest in warmth and kindness, leaving a durable impression on those I encounter.

However, despite my friendly nature, I admit I need support with the art of conversation, looking to find the right words to express myself fully and connect on a deeper level. It is a humble vulnerability that rests within me, as I am excited about learning how to fill the gap between understanding and communication.

To Mr. Grigore Radu Stoian Balaci, a resident of the beautiful commune of -Macesu de Sus; I, soldier Balaci Dumitru, send this heartfelt message.

My dear parents, I pray you to learn of my continued well-being, as I endure the trials of military service. Though I remain distant, and physically separated from you, please rest assured that I am healthy and resilient.

However, the absence of information regarding your circumstances leaves me in a state of uncertainty, desperate to gain any insight into your well-being.

Dear Polina, the depths of my heartache wishing for your presence. As a soldier in service, it has been three arduous years since our last time together. The desire to hold you close and look into your eyes has become an eager ache within me.

Each passing day amplifies my ambition, as the distance between us seems overwhelming. Your absence leaves a void within my soul, and the memories of our love help me every day during my darkest moments.

In the loving moments shared between us, I made a promise that I would return to your side, fascinated by your extraordinary beauty. The idea of being together in our beloved homeland of Romania tempts me, for there lies the home of my beloved parents.

It has been three long years since I last saw their familiar faces and a deep longing stirs within me to find solace once again in their warm arms. By God's grace, I eagerly hope to start the journey that will reunite me with them and grant me the opportunity to see the green fields of my beloved village once more.

The realization of my current situation weighs heavily upon me. I find myself alone and distanced from the calming presence of my dear family. The temptation of foreign lands loses its grip as I yearn for the intimacy of home, the comforting hugs of loved ones, and the simple ways of our Romanian way of life. The prospect of remaining abroad holds little appeal, for my heart beats in unison with the land that raised me, and I am determined in my desire to return to my roots.

The call of Romania resonates deep within me, fuelling my determination to fulfill my promise to you and myself.

With intense hope, I anticipate the day when I shall traverse the miles that separate us, threading my way back to the embrace of my adored family and the embrace of our beloved nation. It is the strength of these connections, rooted in love, that provides me with the courage to navigate the challenges that lie ahead.

In the depths of my being, a sincere desire grows to walk upon the soil of my beloved Romania once again, sunny in its splendor, and be part of our rich cultural heritage.

The desire to be reunited with my loved ones and to immerse myself in the familiar sights, sounds, and scents of our homeland pushes me forward, drawing me fiercely back to the place where my heart finds solace.

With unshakable faith and resolve, I set my sights on the horizon, knowing that the road ahead may be hard. Yet, driven by a love that knows no bounds, I am determined to reclaim my rightful place among my loved ones and within the embrace of our beloved Romania.

January 13, 1919

Today was a day of hard work at the barracks, where I applied myself with full commitment. However, the nature of our work constantly shifts, leaving me uncertain about the specific location and tasks that await me.

Today, it appears that my labour will be directed towards the forest, yet the identities of my fellow workers remain a mystery. In this ever-changing landscape, the only constant seems to be the anticipation of dancing with the lovely girls in the evening.

The allure of dancing with the girls has captured my attention, becoming a source of both excitement and curiosity.

The joy of twirling and swaying to the rhythmic melodies fills my heart with a sense of joy. Last night, I had the pleasure of sharing the dance floor with these captivating ladies, their grace, and beauty leaving a lasting mark on my memory.

Filled with enthusiasm, I extended an invitation to them to visit our barracks, hoping to further receive joy in their presence. However, the prospect of a getting together seemed to overwhelm the girls, as the sheer number of soldiers proved to be a deterrent.

The thought of engaging in lively conversations and forging connections amidst the camaraderie of our comrades appeared to be overshadowed by the potential crowd.

Though their reluctance dampened my spirits momentarily, the resilience within me remains relentless. As I eagerly await the opportunity to return to Romania, my homeland, I find solace in the knowledge that there await a multitude of girls with whom I can engage in profound conversations.

The prospect of reconnecting with familiar faces and engaging in the memorable conversations of my youth fills my heart with anticipation. For now, I bid you farewell, as I navigate the complexities of my current reality, forever hopeful of the eventual reunion with my beloved family.

January 20, 1919

Dearest and beloved parents,

With a heart overflowing with love and concern, I write to assure you that I am in good health and spirits. The circumstances of my current location have kept me at a distance, keeping me ignorant of the realities that unfold within the confines of our beloved home. Oh, how I long for news from our address, yearning to be involved in the details of your lives.

As the sun sets on this eventful day, my thoughts turn eagerly towards tomorrow, where a new chapter awaits me in the captivating embrace of the forest. With each passing dawn, the anticipation grows within me, for it is upon the outlook that I shall venture forth into nature's sanctuary, ready to immerse myself in the tasks that lie ahead.

Intriguingly, amidst the whispers of fate, I have crossed paths with a French rancher. Fate, it seems, has mingled our lives, bonding our destinies in a beautiful friendship. This rancher, with an air of intrigue and a sparkle in his eyes, has expressed a keen interest in my skills and talents.

It is an invitation extended with sincerity and purpose, offering the opportunity to work alongside him and tend to his beloved flock. With will and determination, I step forth to embrace this opportunity for labour. The call of responsibility resonates deep within my being, urging me to contribute my skills and efforts to the task at hand. Though the journey may be challenging and the work demanding, I join this venture with an open heart and a willingness to learn.

Who among us shall partake in this labour? It is I who willingly shoulders this responsibility. Through diligence and dedication, I shall fulfill the duties entrusted to me, seeking to make a meaningful impact in this field of work.

The promise of personal growth and the chance to forge connections with fellow labourers fills my soul with purpose. Oh, how I dream of the day when our paths shall cross once more when I can share tales of my adventures and listen with delighted attention to the stories that have unfolded within the sanctuary of our home. Until then, I send you my love and heartfelt wishes for your well-being.

Yours faithfully, Dumitru

January 29, 1919

My dearest Polina,

As I pen these warm words, an overwhelming wave of sorrow washes over me, for it has been an agonizing three years since the glow of your presence graced my life.

In this vast expanse of time, not a single letter bearing your touch has found its way to my hands, intensifying the ache within my heart.

My heart aches, dear Polina, for the lost moments and the separation endured. I hold adamant to the hope that our paths shall soon meet again, that destiny will work to bring us together once more. Until then, I find solace in the beautiful memories we have created, and the endless love that continues to bind us.

With undying devotion, Dumitru

January 31, 1919

To my beloved family, Mr. Grigore Radu Stoian Balaci,

As I put pen to paper, my heart overflows with longing and concern for each of you. It brings me immense relief to share that I am in good health and spirits, standing strong amidst the trials of this unpredictable journey.

However, the veil of uncertainty obscures my knowledge of the circumstances that unfold within the beloved walls of our home. Oh, how my heart yearns to be surrounded by the familiar embrace of our cherished family.

Three years have passed since our last embrace, and the weight of time has eroded the vivid image of your faces from my memory. Yet, led by the unwavering power of God's grace, I hold the strong hope that our reunion lies on the horizon, awaiting us with open arms.

With each passing day, my longing to see your beloved faces intensifies, for the love that binds us remains sincere and unbreakable. In these moments of reflection, my thoughts reach out to each member of our family. To you, dear Mother and Father, I extend my deepest gratitude for the love and nurturing you have given me. To my dear brothers and sisters, I send my heartfelt regards, longing to once again witness the unbreakable bond that unites us. The memories of our shared laughter and the warmth of our familial love keep me grounded, even as I desire the physical presence of each of you.

Though words cannot fully express the depth of my love and longing, I bid you farewell, for now, my dear family. Rest assured that each passing moment carries me closer to the day when we shall be reunited. Until then, know that you reside in the deepest depths of my heart and that my love for you remains unchanged.

With eternal love, Dumitru

February 3, 1919

On this third day of February, a bitter cold descended upon us, wrapping the world in its icy grip. Our aspirations to venture into the city were thwarted by the unforgiving chill that permeated the air. Wisely, we decided to postpone our journey until the weather granted us a break, for we longed to witness the beauty of the girls who walked the streets. We wished for our efforts to be met with fulfillment, ensuring that our trip would not be in vain.

In the face of such harsh conditions, a thought crossed our minds—to extend an invitation to a young lady, a hope of warmth amidst the frigid night.

We imagined the solace and comfort that would accompany her presence in our humble shack, sharing the protection and affection that only honest care can provide. If we were to go on this trip, we vowed to embrace our role as protectors, cherishing and safeguarding the well-being of our treasured companions.

As I pen these words, I bid you farewell for now. May the coming days bring the promise of milder weather, where our paths may cross with the boundaries of the city and the company of beautiful young ladies.

Until then, let us remain dedicated to our intentions, mindful of the responsibility that accompanies the privilege of sharing our warmth and shelter.

Under the moonlit sky, Soldier Dobre Ion, Ilie, and I embarked on an adventure one evening, our hearts burst with youthful anticipation. Our footsteps carried us through beautiful gardens, a labyrinth of possibilities and potential occurrences.

However, Ilie, ever perceptive, came with a realization—the girls we were looking for were not present in the village. Our hearts sank as the realization dawned upon us; our path came to an abrupt halt, obstructed by the mighty presence of a wandering river. Ion, pondering Ilie's words, urged us to retrace our steps, acknowledging the meaningless pursuit. As we retraced our path, fate played a troublesome hand, and I found myself plunging into a nearby ditch.

The chill of the night air clung to our skin, reminding us of the harsh reality that awaited us. With a heavy heart, Ion proposed that we return to the barracks, accepting the hard truth that the sight of the girls would forever elude us. We lost sleep that night, yearning for a mere illusion.

As we walked back to the barracks, a silent agreement passed among us to leave out tales of our brief encounters with the girls, though the reality was far removed from our shared imagination. Ion, with sadness in his voice, shared that he never had the chance to behold their enchanting presence. In this parting moment, I bid goodbye to the dreams of a passing connection, acknowledging the bitter truth that our paths never truly crossed.

Farewell, my dear, for destiny, kept the joy of our meeting. Though our paths never met, I hold the hope of our missed encounter in my heart, forever embedded in my memories.

February 11, 1919

Yesterday, I joined forces with my admired friend Neacsu Dumitru on a mission to harvest timber on that cold day. Through our combined efforts and determination, we managed to accumulate a good amount of firewood despite the challenging conditions.

Since today's dawn, I have stopped engaging in my regular work duties, as a mandatory directive has been issued forcing us all to take part in the refreshing ritual of bathing. Fear not, for once we have completed our bathing, we shall promptly return to our posts and resume our labours immediately following the midday lunch.

It is my sincere desire to accompany the fair ladies on a delightful stroll through the forest. May they find peace in knowing that we, as individuals of top integrity, pose no threat and only seek to enjoy the beautiful of nature alongside them.

February 12, 1919

With warm affection and longing, I address this letter to my admired parents, beloved brothers, and adored sisters. Allow me to inform you that I am in good health and spirits, yet my heart aches with uncertainty as I remain uncertain of your current well-being.

Nevertheless, I hold intense hope that, by the divine providence of God, our paths shall intersect once more, although the exact moment eludes me. As I find myself deprived of further news to share, I finish this letter as your devoted son, who holds you dear and loves you immensely.

Soldier Dumitru Balaci,
Farewell for now

I seek you to pay attention to the conditions I endured during my arduous stay in Germany. The harsh trials I faced there, inflicted great suffering upon me. Why did I suffer, you may ask?

Hunger, my dear family, hunger tortured me relentlessly, accompanied by a multitude of other hardships. We lived on rations of beetroot soup and putrefied bones. In our desperate circumstances, we resorted to a rather unconventional measure—we set on fire and consumed the putrid bones that had succumbed to decay.

Astonishingly, against all odds, these burnt leftovers appeared strangely appealing, defying their origin in the world of dirt and decay. As we took part in this unorthodox meal, a distinct illusion of goodness came over our senses, momentarily deceiving us into believing that we filled our hunger with an attractive meal. It was an act born out of pure necessity, where even the most disgusting of meals could assume an illusory resemblance of satisfaction.

Now, I find myself fluctuating on the verge of a similar situation, but by the grace of God, I have found consolation in the grasp of our Allied brothers. If it is the divine will, we may yet return to the chest of our homeland, Romania, which we have regrettably allowed to fade from our memory.

Our dear Romania, where our brothers live, is within the embrace of the illustrious Great Romania. Farewell, until we meet again.

> With enduring love and affection,
> Soldier Dumitru Balaci

February 13, 1919

My dearest and beloved Polina,

I implore you to accept this letter as a testament to my lasting love and concern for you. Let it be known that I am in good health and spirits, although the same cannot be said for the state of my heart, burdened by the lack of communication from your side.

Countless words have been dispatched in your name, yet alas, no response has reached my restless hands. If it is the divine will, my beloved mistress, may our paths cross once more soon.

The longing to see you, to be in your presence, has become an all-consuming dream that permeates my nights. It has been far too long since our eyes met, and the ache of that separation grows with each passing day. With no further news to convey, I sign off as your devoted lover. Farewell, my dear child.

February 22, 1919

On this eventful day, we were blessed with the presence of a Romanian priest, who shared with us the wisdom of paternal guidance, instilling in us a renewed sense of purpose and inspiration. His words resonated deeply, offering solace and motivation amidst our trials and tribulations.

Allow me to recommend myself as Soldier Balaci Dumitru, a prisoner who endured the hardships of captivity in Germany. The time spent under the watchful eyes of our adversaries was a miserable existence, like being relentlessly hounded by a ferocious dog. They constantly reminded us of their perceived strength, but we, undeterred, firmly assured them of their certain downfall. And now, as destiny would have it, the German soldiers find themselves at the receiving end of our authority.

To them, I assert with virtuous anger, you are nothing now. By the grace of God, we have found refuge in France, where we no longer bear the chains of captivity but proudly serve as soldiers in the esteemed French Army. Farewell, until we meet again.

Yours faithfully,
Soldier Balaci Dumitru

March 17, 1919

On a serene Sunday, I embarked on a journey to the nearby town. We intended to board the passenger train, but to our surprise, we encountered a freight train instead. Recognizing that this train did not have our village as the destination, I voiced my concern, saying that it was not our intended path. Little did we know that this sudden turn of events would take us to an unfamiliar village, its location was veiled in mystery.

We found ourselves stranded in an unknown place, placed a daunting ten kilometres away from our intended destination. Adamant in our determination, we started the long and arduous journey on foot, for a soldier is free to cross any path that lies before him. These words are inscribed by my hand, capturing the essence of our unexpected adventure.

Oh, Lord, I am asking you to cast your gaze upon the sinful souls that roam beneath the open sky. As I walk this path, I am reminded of my purpose and resilience.

To Mr. Grigore Radu Stoian Balaci, – Macesu de Sus Commune, Dolj County.

From the esteemed sir Balaci Dumitrescu.

My cherished and beloved mistress may my heartfelt wishes reach the depths of your being. *Avirdeizein*.

1919
(exact date unknown)

My dearest and beloved mistress, Catrina, I hold you in the depths of my heart with indescribable love. Yet, I beg you to also keep me in your thoughts, for I find myself trapped in the web of an unforgiving fate.

I wonder, shall I remain in this desolate place? I am but a man who exists in a realm where understanding and communication elude us. I see the depth of your affection, but I am displaced, wanting to find my rightful place.

However, in my prayers, I ask the divine to guide me back to where I belong, for my current existence is that of a bitter prisoner.

Allow me to recommend myself as Soldier Balaci Dumitru, a man of humble education.

Here, in our midst, no one is deprived of the ability to read, for it is a skill we all hold dear.

Reading, my dear Mr. Dumitrescu Balaci, is a precious gift that unifies us all, fostering knowledge and understanding.

I stand in awe of those who possess the ability to share wisdom to me.

March 1919
(Exact Date Unknown)

Today, as the sun casts its warm glow upon us, we embark on a journey to a city in France, the destination shrouded in uncertainty. Our migrant existence continues, with each step leading us from one place to another, rendering us adrift in a sea of unfamiliarity.

The rhythm of constant relocation has left us grappling with a sense of displacement, unsure of where to cling ourselves in this ever-changing environment. For four long months, we have found ourselves stationed in this unknown territory, where the very essence of Paris eludes us.

This beautiful city, renowned for its grandeur and cultural richness, remains a distant dream, an enigma that sparks our curiosity. In this state of transient existence, the desire to discover the marvels of Paris intensifies, yet its elusive nature leaves us wanting to see a glimpse of its greatness.

Amidst the complexities of our circumstances, we find ourselves longing for human connection, a tender touch that is beyond the boundaries of war. However, the pressure imposed upon us denies us the opportunity to create bonds with the fairer sex.

Perhaps it is for the best to tread this path alone, for in a reality where attention is rare, personal pursuits of happiness take precedence as each soldier is left to navigate the solitude that surrounds us, seeking peace in a personal journey.

As we venture forth into this unknown city, we embrace the uncertainties that are laid ahead of us, guided by the hope that in the middle of the unknown, we will discover moments of deep beauty. The road stretches before us, inviting us to soak ourselves in the mysteries that await. Though the company of women may be a distant dream, we march on, creating our paths and moulding our destinies, seeking alleviation in the union of fellow soldiers and the bonds we form along the way.

March 22, 1919

As a soldier, my journey led me to the charming region of Lorena, where I found relief and friendship in the arms of a compassionate family who graciously opened their home to me. From the depths of my being, I formed a sincere attachment to them, seeing them as sub parents during my brief stay there. For two days, I was welcomed with their warm hospitality and experienced moments of pure joy in their company.

Curious about my circumstances as a former prisoner, they asked whether I still carried the burdens of captivity and endured a life of hardship. With warm gratitude, I relayed the news that I am past the confines of imprisonment and now I proudly serve as a soldier in the ranks of the French Army.

Their reply was filled with kindness and compassion, encouraging me to write to them upon my inevitable return to Romania, assuring me that they would write me back.

November 2, 1919

As I sit here, I look back at the journey that took me away from the imprisonment in Germany and Austria, particularly from the city of Salzburg, which was nothing short of a surreal experience.

As we departed, an inexplicable sensation overcame us, almost as if our very eyes were on the verge of popping out. The sky itself seemed to burst into a magnificent display of radiance as if we had emerged from the depths of the earth into a realm of unique wisdom. It was a sight that engraved itself into the depths of our memories, a testament to the liberation we were about to experience.

At precisely 6 o'clock in the evening, a crucial moment developed as we crossed the border into the land of our French brothers. Their presence alone filled our hearts with profound gratitude and joy. Recognizing our disorientation, they generously guided us along the path we should follow, showing us the way with their endless support.

It was an amazing moment for us, as we stood at the crossroads of newfound freedom, uncertain of which direction we should take from there.

With their guidance, we found ourselves making our way towards a quiet village that promised food, comfort, and an opportunity to rebuild our lives.

Arriving at our destination, we were welcomed with open arms, embraced by the warmth of a community that understood the trials we had endured. Food, a nourishment for the body and soul, awaited us, leaving aside the bounds of hunger that had taken over us during our time in captivity. But it was more than just food; it was a symbol of our liberation, a tangible reminder that we were finally liberated from the claws of imprisonment. At that moment, we enjoyed the sweetness of freedom, diving in the friendship and support of our newfound friends.

It was a chapter of our lives where the shadows of captivity gradually faded away, replaced by vibrant hope and new possibilities. The village became our safe place, a place where we could begin to heal the wounds inflicted by our past trials and embrace the promise of a brighter future. As we settled into our newfound freedom, a profound sense of gratitude filled our hearts. We were no longer prisoners; we were free souls, connected by shared experiences and an unshakable determination to rebuild our lives.

The journey had led us from the depths of imprisonment to the verge of newfound perspective, and we would forever carry the memories of that transformative moment, carved deeply within our souls.

Dumitru

Epilogue

In the last entry of his journal, Dumitru ends his narrative with a captivating tale. Unfortunately, the precise details of his escape and journey to the French border remain undisclosed on these pages. The fate of these prisoners and the challenges they faced while risking their lives for freedom across the border remain largely unknown.

Soldier Dumitru Balaci, a remarkable individual whose life spanned from 1893 to 1979, leaves behind a legacy that continues to thrive through generations. His memory is lovingly preserved by his two granddaughters, born in the years 1953 and 1956, who carry forth the values he instilled within them.

Over time, the Balaci lineage has flourished, with Dumitru's descendants multiplying into a beautiful family. The reflection of his existence resounds through the lives of his seven great-grandchildren: six wonderful great-granddaughters and a spirited great-grandson. Beyond the great-grandchildren, the Balaci family tree extends further, reaching the realm of great-great-grandchildren- These little ones, brimming with life and potential, represent the future chapters of the Balaci descendants, maintaining the seeds of resilience and strength spread by their remarkable ancestors.

The love, dedication, and permanent impact of Dumitru's life can be witnessed in the seven great-grandchildren and six great-great-grandchildren, perpetuating his memory, the values he held dear, and the rich tale of his family's history. The legacy of Soldier Dumitru Balaci extends far beyond his time on this earth, his descendants continue to flourish and multiply, and his spirit lives on through these new generations.

Dumitru Balaci (1983–1979), affectionately known as Bâte within the family, found his final resting place in – Macesu de Sus cemetery, located in the central area under the shade of a walnut tree, among other hundreds of members of the Balaci family.

He belonged to a sizable family, with Gheorghita and Dumitru Grigore Balaci as his parents. The family included a total of five sons and a daughter. While the exact birth order of Dumitru is unknown, his strong commitment and responsibility towards his family were evident. This commitment led to his strong desire to return to Romania when the opportunity arose.

Upon his return to Romania, approximately around 1920–1921, Dumitru's life took an unexpected turn. His first marriage, to Stana, was marked by tragedy, and he became a widower. They had established a family of two children (a son and a daughter) when, unfortunately, Stana, in her 30s, contracted an illness and passed away prematurely. However, in 1936–1937, a new chapter unfolded, as he remarried my great-grandmother, Floarea Burnea, and together, they welcomed their daughter, Ioana, on the 15th of May 1937.

To follow in the footsteps of Dumitru and discover an unknown world, I embarked on a journey to the village of his birth. The experience was profound as I paid my respects at his resting place. The surprise came when I realized that the house of his birth and the cemetery where he found eternal rest were practically neighbours—just a couple of steps apart.

From the yard of his childhood home, a simple peek over the fence revealed the distant cemetery—a sentimental reminder of Dumitru's final resting place. The place radiated a special essence that was imprinted in my heart. A later exploration with my sisters led us to the discovery that beneath the shelter of this walnut tree in the cemetery, countless members of the Balaci family lay peacefully side by side. The discovery that he was surrounded by his parents, siblings, brothers-in-law, cousins, and grandchildren unfolded a part of the family I never knew existed.

The deep connection to our roots in the village made me dig deeper into the history of -Macesu de Sus. In my research, I discovered that the village had its foundations laid between the years 1500–1600, with a rich agricultural history.

Dumitru, a craftsman by trade, neatly worked as a fur coater and seamstress, creating a variety of coats. At the same time, he tended to agriculture, cultivating corn, wheat, and watermelon following local customs. His resourceful role reflected a dedication to both his craft and the land, a testament to the resilience and productive spirit that defined him.

Dumitru's unshakable faith was a defining trait that shaped his life from an early age. This commitment was inscribed in his journal, a testament to his surviving spirit during the terrifying times he spent in war camps, transported back and forth as a captive in Germany and Austria.

His faith wasn't merely a passive trait; it served as a guiding force, a constant ally that pushed him forward in the face of adversity. Through the trials and tribulations of captivity, fuelled by his faith and deep-rooted desire to return home and build a family, he found the strength to endure the harshest conditions.

The desire to draw his last breath at home and be laid to rest beside his family in the village cemetery was a dire wish that became a reality, living on until the wonderful age of 86. In the upcoming years, Dumitru embraced a peaceful life alongside his wife and daughter.

During the hectic era of the Second World War, he proudly served his country. When French Allied soldiers entered the Romanian territory, Dumitru, with an immense sense of pride, engaged in lengthy conversations and assisted them. This act of camaraderie mirrored the warmth he experienced in France, a nation that welcomed him with open arms after his challenging escape from the prison camp in Salzburg, Germany.

Cherished memories stayed in the hearts of my mom and aunt, who recall with a smile the visits of their grandfather Dumitru, residing in a neighbouring village merely seven kilometres away. While today, seven kilometres may seem like an unimportant distance easily covered in a short car ride, it symbolizes a profound connection to the past. Close to a century ago, when Dumitru finally returned home, he started a ritual that would not only shape his life but also set the stage for a lasting family history.

Twice a week, on Thursdays and Sundays, Dumitru and his wife Floarea went on a journey covering a 14 kilometres round trip to reach the small church in a neighbouring village called Goicea, where their daughter Ioana lived alongside her husband Ion and their daughters (my mother included). The simplicity of their lives was obvious—they lacked the luxury of a carriage or a bicycle, and in those long-gone days, owning a car was not even an option. Not moved by the weather, they travelled the distance faithfully, whether rain, blizzard, or sunshine, to attend the sermons from the pulpit of our cherished little church.

As the family expanded, so did the traditions. Following church, my mother and aunt distinctly remember how they would join Dumitru and Floarea on their journey, spending time together and bonding. These post-church visits to my grandparents' home next door became cherished moments, a blend of familial warmth and spiritual feed.

My aunt, with a spark of pride in her eyes, remembers countless days when he held her and her sisters on his knees after the church service. In those intimate moments, he shared tales of his wartime experiences, speaking with pride about his survival and learning of the French language. The pride mirrored in Dumitru's eyes during these moments was immeasurable—a testament to the resilience and strength that defined the family through generations, sewed together by the threads of love, faith, and shared history.

Dumitru's wisdom, hardened from a life rich in experiences and adversity, became a precious legacy passed down through each generation in our family—a beacon of guidance that resonates through family history. His counsel, profound and timeless, has not only endured but has been embraced by each of us, shaping our perspectives and choices. Among the words of wisdom he shared, none was brighter than his insistence on us travelling, to see the world beyond our small village. He passionately encouraged us to go into the wider world, insisting that opportunities for growth, knowledge, and self-realization shine beyond the familiar borders of our rural area. This advice, a call to explore, learn, and broaden our horizons, echoed in our ears and sparked curiosity within our hearts.

Central to his teachings was the significance of education. Dumitru, very aware of the transformative power of knowledge, highlighted the importance of reading books, pursuing studies, and acquiring the skills necessary to navigate the complexities of life. His belief in the transformative potential of education stemmed not only from its practical utility but also from the belief that a wealthy mind could resist the challenges of an ever-evolving world.

The essence of his advice, however, was a profound lesson collected from the melting pot of war—an insight that etched itself into the core of our familial mentality. Life, he stressed, is naturally fleeting, and the echoes of war taught him a certain truth: the consciousness of existence necessitates a life lived without regrets. Every opportunity, he begged, must be seized with action and purpose. To achieve greatness in life, one must not merely exist but actively take the opportunities that unfold before them.

In shifting these teachings into the fabric of our lives, Dumitru's legacy continues to inspire, guiding us towards a future marked by resilience, a thirst for knowledge, and a commitment to seize every chance to realize our fullest potential. The echoes of his advice resonate with time, a lasting testament to the enduring impact of wisdom passed down from one generation to the next.

Dumitru, a man of humble beginnings and gentle spirit, left a lasting mark on our family with his simple yet profound gestures. Among the sweetest memories were the treats he brought for his granddaughters—although, in those times, desserts were no more than candies at best. Despite the simplicity of these offerings, his granddaughters eagerly anticipated his visits each week, excitedly awaiting the chance to spend cherished moments in his company.

Dumitru's physical appearance, with his tall, thin frame and big blue eyes, told a tale of both external and internal scars, a testament to the trials he faced. Yet, within him beat a heart of gold, filled with eternal love for his family and country. His character, shaped by life's hardships, radiated warmth and resilience.

As the visits ended, Dumitru, in his gentle way, took on the role of a storyteller and contemplation. He would tuck the girls into bed, telling stories that transcended generations and sharing small pieces of wisdom. He encouraged his granddaughters never to go to bed with unresolved conflicts, asking them to seek forgiveness if wronged and try to mend any tension.

The wish to have met him, to share a moment, or offer a comforting hug, echoes through the years. Though the opportunity to cross paths was not possible by the limits of time, my soul finds solace in knowing that I carry his legacy within me.

Dumitru's influence, far from confined to fleeting moments, endures through the pages of his treasured journal. The inheritance he left, though intangible, is priceless, and his blood runs through my veins, a silent testament to the sacrifices and struggles he has been through. Born a few years after his passing, I am granted the privilege to tell his story, a story knitted with threads of resilience, love, and the invincible human spirit.

In possessing this journal, a profound connection is forged— a link to a past where captivity threatened lives, and not all emerged without scars. Dumitru's words passed through time, uncovering a diversity of experiences that, while not unique, stand as a testament to the enduring power of the human spirit in the face of difficulty.

Acknowledgments

I extend my heartfelt gratitude and admiration to my mother, who faithfully safeguarded her grandfather's war journal over time.

It is through her unwavering commitment to preserving our family's history that we have been granted the privilege of embarking on this profound journey.

I must also express my sincere appreciation to my beloved sisters, whose unwavering support and encouragement have propelled me forward in giving our great-grandfather's journal the voice it deserves.

Together, we have embarked on a mission to honour his memory and ensure that his experiences are not forgotten.

In the depths of this journal, written by the hand of soldier Dumitru Balaci himself, lies an invaluable treasure. It serves as a testament to his indomitable spirit and a testament to his unwavering determination to overcome the insurmountable challenges that stood in his path.

Through his meticulous documentation of the hardships he endured, he provides us with a glimpse into a world long gone, yet one that reverberates with resonance even to this day. His words, etched on those fragile pages, transcend time and space, allowing us to hear his voice echo from beyond the grave.

His determined courage and resilience in the face of unimaginable difficulty continue to inspire me. It is through his words that I strive to convey the magnitude of his war experience, allowing you, the reader, to walk alongside him on his arduous path.

In this act of sharing his war experiences, I am acutely aware that the gift entrusted to me extends far beyond the pages of this book.

The greatest gift is the gift of life itself, and it is only through the grace of God that I stand here today, able to bring Dumitru Balaci's story to light. It is with deep humility and profound gratitude that I embarked on this journey, hoping to honour his memory and preserve the legacy he left behind.

Printed in the USA
CPSIA information can be obtained
at www.ICGtesting.com
LVHW092311100524
779795LV00002B/191

9 781038 309280